Smile When You

Feel Like Dying

Author Joanna

Smile When You Feel Like Dying

To Contact the Author
e-mail ban0128@yahoo.com

Front Cover @2006 by PaTricia Arnold

ISBN: 978-0-6151-3922-7

Acknowledgments

My first "thank you" goes to PaTricia, my wonderful daughter who gave her time up at the computer to allow me time to finish this book.

More thanks goes to the following people for all their encouragement to me that kept me focused on finishing this book: my three sons, John, Robert, Craig, and John's wife Jennifer.

My cousins, Heather, and Travis and others such as Julia, Lori, and my long lost extra son, "Shane", and many others who read my blog and left comments.

Thank you Tina for being my friend through it all. Thank you for believing in me.

Thank you Lisa, my co-worker who read my book and encouraged me that this story can help other women who are going through the same things.

Thank you Shawn for holding my hand when I needed it the most.

Last but not least I want to thank my mom for praying for me. Without her love and prayers I am not sure where I would be in my life. She has been my constant during my tumultuous life. Thank you mom!

You all have encouraged me to go forward with this book and getting my story out to the other people who can be encouraged from my life story.

PREFACE

Please do not read this book until you have first read the preface. This is a story of my life, as I know it. It contains the good, the bad, and the ugly parts of what happened to me throughout my life, mainly focusing on the time of my life through the divorce and after. The words written in this book are important for me to share in order to complete my healing.

I was living my life wearing a mask. The people who knew me saw me smiling. They had no idea of the pain that I was feeling inside. People around us had no idea of the abuse that was happening in our home. We lived a lie.

When I finally decided it was time for me to break away from the lies and the marriage my life spiraled out of control. I sought solace in places I had never been and lived a life that I knew nothing about before that time in my life. At one time, I tried to kill myself believing it would be better for my family.

My family turned from me believing the lies and accusations that my husband told them. Some of the incidents that happened were not an end all of relationships. Although it appeared that I had nobody to turn to as I faced accusation after accusation.

As of the time of this writing, many of the relationships were healed with time. I am close again to my mother and other family members as I strive to grow closer to God these relationships have been healed. As for my children, I do not know what I would do without them. John and Robert, my oldest sons, continue to be a source of strength as they have grown into great men and fathers themselves. The trying times we had during the divorce are but a memory and my prayer is that the demons that existed during that time have moved on to other topics that are not raised in my family today.

The feelings I had at that time were just that, my feelings. I do not hold grudges against those people who had good intentions although I was unable to see their good intentions for the trauma that I was facing.

I have grown with time since the divorce and I do forgive Arnold for the things that we went through. I am happy he has found someone in his life to whom he can give his love and life to. My prayer is that he will remain a good companion to her throughout their lives. My prayer is that he has learned through trials and tribulations and a loss of a marriage, patience.

All credit is given to God who gave me strength to go through the hard times and come out on the other end with purpose and meaning in life.

Currently I am attending the University of Central Oklahoma pursuing a Bachelor's Degree in Political Science. I have my own business, Easy Paralegal Services (www.easyparalegalservices.com) which was set up to help many people in their legal struggles without the high cost of an attorney. My future goal is to attend Law School and become an attorney. I want to be able to help other women with their legal battles in order to free themselves from the demons in their lives.

CHAPTER 1

In 1997, it appeared that we were such a happy family, my husband, four kids, and I. We were having a few problems with the kids but overall they were great kids. I was smiling! The sun was shining and we were on our way back to Springfield, Missouri for Arnold to attend graduate school at Baptist Bible College.

My dream for our family was for Arnold to pastor a church, as I believed that's what God wanted from our family.

We had been through many trials throughout our marriage. Arnold had faced, and it appeared that he had conquered many demons, which had haunted him in the past. He had been abusive from the beginning of our marriage both mentally and physically.

We were leaving Oklahoma City where my husband had been assistant pastor for two years with our friend and mentor Bro. Eddis. It was the day before Memorial Day 1997, the church threw us a 'going away' party.

We had so many friends and family at our church. We were leaving a church we had been members of since the kids were toddlers. We were leaving a church that ministered to most of my family members. I had learned more about God and his Word in that church and was looking forward to what the future held. We all knew that God had used us in a great way while we were there.

Monday morning was Memorial Day, we finished packing the truck to make the trip to Springfield. When we arrived in Springfield, it appeared Arnold was happy with the world. It had been somewhat a strain in Oklahoma because the church we were in had many problems that needed to be dealt with, however, instead of dealing with the problems, most of them had been swept under the rug.

I began working full-time when we were in Bible College the first time in 1991 so Arnold could focus on his schooling. In 1993 I decided to stop homeschooling the boys and attend school full time in order to get my Associates Degree. In 1995, Arnold graduated Bible

College with his Bachelor's Degree in Theology and I graduated with my Associates Degree.

Arnold wanted to go back to Oklahoma City to work with the man who had led him to Christ. I did not think it was the best idea but I reluctantly agreed to go back to Oklahoma. I would have to continue to work full time so that he could spend more time at the church. The church could not pay him much only $100.00 per week but the duties had required him to work full-time. Arnold wanted to 'fix' the church. We saw many people hurting and tried to minister to them during that time. I worked full time and spent many evenings and most of the weekends working beside him at the church.

We had no idea that our pastor, friend and mentor was as sick as he was. He had been in the hospital a few times during those two years but we believed he would get better and everything would be all right. He had made some decisions that we could not agree with and was out of his character to make such decisions.

Several church members came to our home to ask Arnold to take the church as pastor or to start another church in Oklahoma City. We knew we could not hurt our pastor, friend, and mentor so we made the decision to leave. We believed that our leaving would stop the contentions that were in the church at that time.

During Bible College the Professors had drilled in our heads, that a church split would benefit nobody so our decision was to return to Springfield.

We arrived in Springfield, and spent the rest of the week unpacking and reacquainting ourselves with old friends. Arnold went to the college and enrolled in the graduate program only to find out that we were short of funds and he would have to take out student loans to go to school.

Arnold began to get discouraged. I loved him so much and I was trying to ease the pain by encouraging him to go ahead and attend the graduate program. I informed him that God was in control and he would help meet our needs.

I told him that I would continue to work full time somewhere so that he could focus on school. We had been in Springfield only 4 days. I remember sitting in the living room and we were talking about what we should do regarding graduate school when the phone rang.

"Joanna" ... You could hear it in my mom's voice when I answered the phone that she was shaken up about something big.

I began crying before she even said it.

"I have some good and bad news, and I will say it all in one sentence".

She paused and I could hear her sobbing.

"Bro. Eddis went to Heaven."

I stood there holding the phone, not sure that I heard her correctly then I didn't want to believe her, I felt my body shaking, my lips quivering, tears flowing like they would never stop.

This was the man that God sent to my life when I needed him most.

This was the man I called when I was having problems with my last pregnancy with my daughter and my husband would not take me to the hospital to get my pain shot. When Bro. Eddis arrived at my house he saw me lying on the ground and Arnold was standing over me. He barely put the car in park and ran up the hill of my front yard because he thought Arnold had hit me. He put up his fists to Arnold and said, "Come on! Hit me!"

I could not get the words out fast enough that I was on the ground because I was having a labor pain. Arnold had decided to take me to the hospital after I had called Bro. Eddis.

This was the man that during one of our weekly counseling sessions knocked Arnold out of the chair in his office when Arnold did not believe he was wrong in hitting me.

This man knelt down at the altar with Arnold and led him to Christ.

This was the man who tried to let God be in charge of it all, who would always ask the question, "What does the Bible say?"

This was the man whom I loved and who loved everyone he met.

This was also the man who no longer was in pain, who no longer had worries, who was able to kiss this world goodbye.

I could go on and on with what man this was to me. However, at that moment I found out that this was the man able to walk on the streets of gold and not look back.

Packing for the trip back to Oklahoma City for the funeral was difficult, the tears would not stop. All the times he helped me in my life flooded my head. The memories of what he had meant to my family were overwhelming. No more could he drive all the way to Springfield while he was sick because he wanted to be there to help us in our marriage. No more could I call him when things were bleak. I felt that not only had I lost a friend but had lost the one person in the world who wanted to see us fulfill our dreams and wanted to see our marriage which was destined to fail, survive.

We made the trip back to Oklahoma to attend his funeral. The church he had pastored for over 20 years was full and overflowing. Every Sunday school class was full of people there were several closed circuit televisions set up in every class in the church. He was such a humble man who helped shape so many lives. I wondered if he even knew what an impact that he had on so many people. I could honestly sing the song, "Thank you for Giving to the Lord" to this man.

I watched his wife say goodbye to her husband and knew that she helped shape this man who has meant so much to our family. I hurt for her.

After the funeral, Arnold advised the men of the church that he wanted to be a candidate for pastor of the church. The response was that he had moved to Springfield so that he could attend Graduate School and Bro. Eddis would have wanted him to finish that. Therefore, they would not accept his application.

This sent Arnold into a deep depression; he never attended graduate school. The week we returned to Springfield Arnold went back up to the school and withdrew from his classes. I tried to help but instead I was just in his way.

His depression was too deep; the what-ifs were too many. What if we had not left Oklahoma, what if Bro. Eddis had not died, what if, what if, and what if.

My idea was that we went through Bible College to be in the ministry so I wrote our resume and mailed it to every church that was seeking a pastor. I was going to help him overcome, I wanted us to make our dreams come true.

My hope was that he would come back to a place in his life that he wanted to be in the ministry.

Churches began calling, some just wanted a preacher to fill in on Sunday while their pastor was away.

Some of the churches were actually calling to schedule interviews.

Arnold responded to each call and we would go to each church that called.

I began to see a glimmer in his eyes that maybe things were going to get better for him.

CHAPTER 2

Arnold was preaching again. We were traveling all over Missouri, Oklahoma and Kansas candidating for churches. Arnold was preaching and I was singing.

It looked as if that was what God wanted from us. We were candidating at a church in Ozark, Missouri when the people asked if they could take the vote to make him pastor. Arnold told them okay. The men told him they would call him tonight when they were finished. We went home and they called us about an hour later.

"We want you to be our pastor" I heard as I was on the other line.

Yay! I thought . . .

Until I heard him say,
"I can't take the position right now."

WHAT?! I wanted to say it out loud in the receiver but the voice was not there.

This was the first of 3 callings that Arnold turned down. The other one was in Kansas and one was in Southern Oklahoma.

On the way back from Kansas after he turned that calling down we got into a heated argument on the way home, he pulled the car over and made me get out. I don't know how long it was or how far I walked but he finally came back tears on his face and he began to tell me how sorry he was for what he did.

We got home and he grabbed all the resumes, tore them up, and told me to quit being his Holy Spirit. He told me that God did not want him to pastor and that he would just continue to work in the bus barn at Baptist Temple in Springfield.

I was working at a telephone company and was working a lot of overtime. I needed that break from everything at home. Arnold could not say anything nice to the kids or me and I just wanted to escape the negativism. I was the auditor and the liaison between our company and Southwestern Bell. If I saw accounts that had been overcharged, I was able to credit their accounts to make it accurate. I was respected at my job and held a lot of responsibility.

The kids were growing up and learning to make decisions on their own. My sons John, Robert and Craig were all working at Arby's . . . Honestly, I know Trish was around there somewhere but she was spending a lot of time by herself.

I felt guilty about all that but I had to work and work I did. Most weeks I put in 65+ hours at work. When I got home I was exhausted but still had a lot of work to do, laundry, cooking, cleaning and doing whatever Arnold told me to do. I hated my life, everything about it. I hated myself, I hated Arnold, I hated my house, I hated my church, and yes I hated God. Why would he do this to us?

We lived like this for 2 years just surviving. Arnold working at the bus barn at our church 'Baptist Temple' and we were teaching Sunday school and the class was growing. Nobody knew what was going on behind closed doors at our home. I had learned from Bro. Eddis to smile and 'pretend' all was okay with life, so that I did. I didn't have a close enough friend to talk to about what was really going on in our home.

"What do you mean I didn't iron that right?"

"How am I suppose to cook a 4 course meal every night when I don't even get home from work before 7:00 every night?"

I would question things I was told to do every time I was told to do something. I had become one of the kids. If it wasn't done correctly there was hell to pay. I paid a lot of hell.

I did not know what it felt like for my ribs or the back of my legs not to hurt because they did all the time. If it wasn't from being slapped, it was from being pushed upstairs to my bedroom so that I could be shoved around, knocked to the ground and kicked in the ribs.

I hated that bedroom.

I hated HIM.

I wanted to die!

That was my only way out and I knew it. I learned to put on a 'face on' for church and for people who would come around. I smiled yet it was fake because I only felt like dying on the inside.

If Arnold thought I was talking to someone about what was going on in our home he would forbid me from seeing or talking to him or her without his being present. I would see them at church and that would be it. I couldn't tell anyone because he promised me I would not live to tell another person. I was so afraid.

One of our friends was in the graduate program at the college and was in his final year. He had an assignment to do which required him to find a married couple to take a personality test. Arnold and I took the personality test and scored on opposite ends of the spectrum. He scored the highest you could score in the dominant category. I scored as high as you could possibly score on the submissive category. I wasn't shocked about that but our friend was. This started yet another fight between us. Arnold claimed that I had lied on the test we took to make him look bad. I claimed that his dominance was the problem we were having in our marriage.

There were enough final straws to end it a long time before I did. However, for the kids, for the religion, and for the dreams we had shared and for the love that I once had for this man, I stuck it out.

"I'm spending a week at camp cooking, you better behave yourself while I am gone." He told me before he left for camp.

"Yeah whatever." I thought to myself.

While he was gone, I planned how I was going to end this 18 year long marriage I was in.

I got on the Internet, found a divorce support group, and began sharing my story with strangers on the Internet. Their advice was that I either get out by leaving or get out by his hands killing me. I didn't really know what to do.

I tried to pray but somehow I felt God didn't even care about me. I was still reading my Bible everyday trying to figure out if God really did care about my situation. On Thursday before Arnold got home from camp I was reading my daily Bible Study and God completely showed me what I had to do.

Proverbs 26:21 "As coals are to burning coals, and wood to fire; so is a contentious man to kindle strife." Arnold had caused so much strife and contention in our home it was time for me to move on.

I decided that it was best to romance him when he came home and then allow God to work through what needed to be done. So the weekend he got home we were like newlyweds. I pretended to be happy he was home and showered him with love.

Sunday was my birthday so we all went out to dinner after church. After church he decided to do some work around the yard. Something set Arnold off. He had asked Craig and Trish to do something in the backyard. They got into a fight and both of them came in the house. Arnold became so angry with Craig that he pushed him into a wall and hit him. Then he told Craig to leave and never come back. All the good that happened over the weekend was lost.

He and Craig had had several problems between them. A few weeks earlier Craig had ditched church. Arnold came into church to get me to go with him to find Craig. We found him at home and Arnold made him do the dishes. Craig did not want to do the dishes so he was just rinsing them and throwing them in the sink. Arnold grabbed the dishes and threw them back in the sink for Craig to wash. Craig reached into the sink and pulled out a knife. I was sitting on the sofa watching the two of them yell at each other before I realized that Arnold had jumped backwards. Craig was holding the knife to Arnold's heart. My first instinct was to tell Craig to go ahead and kill him. Craig was yelling at his dad telling him he was sick of everything he had done to our family. I stood up and walked over to Craig and calmly told Craig to put the knife down this was not the way to handle this situation. Craig put the knife in the sink and began crying uncontrollably. Arnold shoved us both into the wall and went to the phone and called the police. The police came and interviewed all three of us separately. They told Arnold that he was the one who caused the outburst and that they were not taking Craig anywhere.

The problems with Arnold and Craig became unbearable even after we took Craig to the Psychologist. During one of our family meetings, the Psychologist told me that Craig was not the problem but his father was. I didn't know what to do.

Now Arnold had told Craig to leave forever and not to come back. I had no control over it. He was only 15 years old.

Arnold came into the bedroom where I had been working as I often brought work home. He began telling me that I had failed in raising our kids. He told me that I was a bad influence on the kids and then he threw in, I WILL find out who you slept with while I was gone. What? I had not cheated on him, I would have been too afraid to cheat on him. What was he talking about? He left the room to go see about Trisha.

I took the opportunity to get back on the Internet with my divorce support people I had chatted with the week while he was gone. I was also working from home so when he came in the room I would close out the screen and go back to working.

He came in and said he wanted to see what I was typing. I pulled it up only to click on the x in the right corner of the screen and close the page before he saw what I was typing. He threw my work around the room and then grabbed my hair and began slamming my head into the table where the computer was sitting.

He started screaming at me that someone was going to die tonight and it isn't going to be me. Something rose up inside of me –

"WELL IT ISN'T GONNA BE ME EITHER!"

I stood up and shoved him back screaming at him.

"WHO DO YOU THINK YOU ARE? YOU WILL NEVER TOUCH ME AGAIN! GET OUT OF MY HOUSE!"

Something, I don't know what it was but something happened to me that night. I learned that he was weak. That he was scared. He began crying. Oh no, that will not work this time.

He did leave. I learned later that he slept in his car at the bus barn where he worked at the church. I was elated that this marriage might just be over now. However, I had no idea of the actual hell I would fall into because of this.

CHAPTER 3

The first week he was gone was tough. I didn't know whom to talk to or whom I could turn to so that I could talk about the situation. I did not want the kids to be involved in the process or what was going on in our divorce so I wouldn't talk to them or anyone else except people on the internet about my situation. I continued to work but tried to cut my hours spent at work down to the minimum by bringing more work home with me to complete.

We had talked about and planned our first family vacation before I threw him out. He called me every day asking and begging me to take him back and for us to get back together. I told him our marriage was over but if he promised that he would treat me nice then I would agree to this family vacation.

We agreed that we both wanted this to be an amicable split so we decided to go ahead and take this family vacation. I figured that since I had stood up to him he would not hurt me again.

We planned to spend a couple of days in St Louis and then go elsewhere. The boys wanted to go to Ohio to some theme park up there. We knew we did not have enough money to do that so we just planned to stay in St Louis and go to Six Flags and maybe to the zoo or other places and then we were going to drive to Oklahoma to announce the pending divorce to the family.

We left on vacation and Arnold had this brilliant idea to stop at a park by a river to 'talk'. He began telling the kids that we were getting divorce. What a stupid idea – yeah tell the kids before the vacation begins that this will be the first and last family vacation we had ever been on as a family.

I just sat there at that table in the park speechless at the words I was hearing. The looks on the kids faces were of astonishment – what were they feeling at that moment? The crushing blow of a ball and chain hitting their hearts knowing that their mom and dad's destiny was not what they had envisioned prior to this moment.

We did go to St Louis and Arnold and I took time to talk about the best way to finalize this amicably. It was actually a good trip considering what loomed before us when we returned to Springfield.

We had agreed that we would go to an attorney together or I would go to an attorney and then he would just sign the papers and it would be less costly. He had agreed to my keeping the house and the van we had bought a couple of months before. He agreed the kids would stay with me.

John and Robert were going to begin their senior year in high school and he seemed more than willing to pay the child support since it would only be a year with four children. I advised him that I really didn't need much child support since the three older boys were working and I had this full time job I could easily make ends meet without his help.

We went on to Oklahoma and made the announcement to family that we were splitting up. I to this day do not think many people believed us. However, Arnold had admitted he did not treat me 'right' without going into detail he told family members that he felt I would be happier with someone else in my life.

Little did I know that this ended up being for his benefit for future reference. We returned to Springfield. He wanted to stay at the house until he could find a small apartment I didn't think that was a good idea and told him that I would give him one night at the house so that he could gather all his stuff and find somewhere to stay.

The next morning he gathered his stuff and I watched him drive off. I had no idea where he was going to stay I just knew it was not a good idea for him to remain in the house. I made some calls to apply for Legal aid to obtain an attorney and that went through quickly since I knew several people at the financial aid office, and I had an appointment with an attorney for the next day.

The next morning I woke up and found Arnold sitting on the edge of my bed crying. He said he was sorry for everything and he didn't want this divorce to go through. I told him that it was better for both of us to part ways. He said he wouldn't do it without a fight. I don't know what caused his change of attitude, just the day before he seemed fine with everything and was more than willing to work through the things that needed to be worked through.

I told him we didn't need to fight about it. He said 'I know you have someone else in your life and you just want me out so you can move him in'. No, I didn't have anyone else in my life. I just wanted out of the hell I had been in during our marriage. I told him to get out and he advised me that he would do anything in his power to make me look like the bad person.

I told him nobody had to be the bad person that we could work this out without anything coming out about what was really happening in our home. He left after an argument reminding me that I was put on this earth to be obedient to him only and that he would always be my husband. I tried to remain calm and advised him not for too much longer I would not be his wife and I didn't have to do what he said any more.

I met with the attorney and he was going to draw up the paperwork as I asked and that I could prepare most of the pleadings. He gave me a disk with several different types of divorces and the child support with the guidelines so that I could type them up at home.

I returned home and decided that I wanted to relax in the tub for a while. I was sitting in the tub when I heard someone in the house. The kids had started school and nobody should be in the house.

I started to get out of the tub when I heard Arnold calling for me. I hollered back that I was in the tub. He opened the bathroom door and I saw the look on his face was not a good look. He told me that he would not sleep in the bus barn at the church for another night and that this was his home and he was going to stay there whether I liked it or not.

I told him that this was not happening and he had to leave. He said over my dead body that he wouldn't be leaving this house. He tried to shove me down in the tub and I wrestled with him while in the water he managed to dunk me underwater and leave me there long enough that I thought I was going to drown. I knew I had to get out of that tub!

I managed to maneuver myself in such a way to get out from under his grip and I was able to get out of the tub. I ran out the door and outside and around the house to the front door and ran to the telephone.

It wasn't until I was on the phone with 9-1-1 that I realized I didn't even have a towel around my naked body. He was banging at the front door and I was afraid. I yelled to him that I was on the phone with the police and they were on their way.

The operator told me to stay on the line until police arrived I advised her that I was naked and needed to get some clothes on before the police got there. I laid the telephone down with her still on the telephone and ran upstairs to my bedroom and grabbed a bathrobe and ran to the back door and locked it then I ran back down the stairs to the telephone.

On my way downstairs I saw Arnold leaving as he was spinning his wheels out of the driveway. I told the 9-1-1 operator that it was all right that he had gone and I hung up the telephone while being told to stay on the line. Within minutes, the police were there. I spoke to the police and the first thing they told me was that I needed to obtain a restraining order against him.

As soon as the police left I went downtown to the District Court and filed a restraining order against Arnold. I had hoped it would not come to this and that we could be friends while going through this ordeal.

I decided to go by my work since I had been off work almost 2 weeks. I just wanted to see what was going on. I walked into the office and one of my co-workers called me in her office. She said that they had found some discrepancies and were going to have to let me go.

I had done wrong. I had been crediting my telephone account so that my bill would not be so high and had been found out. It was my fault and my doing and I deserved to be let go.

The general manager and my boss came in and told me what they had found. I was so disappointed in myself that I had stooped to such a low thing but at the time I didn't know what to do.

They advised me they would still give me a good reference and that other than this I had been a good employee. I could not stop crying. I told them I was also going to be going through a divorce and my life was in shambles now.

They told me they would keep me on as if I had not lost my job so that I could keep the insurance as long as I paid for the insurance the next month. I would not be paid but I needed to get a psychologist.

They gave me a check for severance pay, which included a month of pay. They did not have to do that since the reason for my being fired was my own doing.

I left there feeling numb and walked down to the Family Services office to file for food stamps and any other help they could give me. I sat there and watched the people around me. I did not belong here I had managed on my own without help from the state.

I wasn't poor but I wasn't rich either, I had no idea what would happen while I sat there waiting for the social worker to call my name.

The time sitting there allowed me time to think about the situation I was in and what I should do next.

I went into a small room and sat down on the opposite side of the table from the social worker. She sat there and looked at the form I had filled out before being called back.

She scratched her head and asked me if that was an accurate amount of pay for my household. I told her it was. She informed me that the amount of money that was brought into the home was too much for Family Services to be able to help. I advised her that I had just lost my job and was not sure how long it would take me to find another job.

I informed her that I was going through a divorce. Nothing I said would faze her. She tried in her feeble attempt to console me. I'm sorry about your divorce. After a couple of months if you still have not found employment come back to see us and then maybe we can help you.

I walked back to my car feeling even more defeat. As I walked toward the van parked on the side of the street the numbness and loneliness seemed to overtake me. As I walked closer to my van I saw something under my windshield wiper. I walked up to my van and noticed I had been issued a parking ticket.

This was the darkest day of my entire life.

Joanna

CHAPTER 4

I believed the only way for my kids to be safe and for Arnold to be free was for me to take my own life.

I got in my van, drove to I-65, and revved the engine up to a speed of about 80-mph. I saw a tree in the distance and decided that if I hit the tree then it would all be over, my hell would be gone and I would be in heaven. I could talk to Bro. Eddis and kneel at the feet of Jesus asking him for his forgiveness. It would be the best thing for everyone concerned.

None of what had happened in our home would ever leak out and Arnold could still preach as if nothing were wrong. I would not have ruined anyone's lives; I would be saving their lives!

So I headed for the tree. I was off the highway and still driving at a very high rate of speed.

As I neared the tree I saw in front of me my first born son, John begging me,

"Mom, NO you can't do this!"

Then Robert,

"No mom we need you!"

Then Craig,

"I love you mommy"

And finally Trisha telling me,

"Mom, you gave me life, don't take yours" . . .

All three of the kids were crying.

I saw the tree still coming toward me. I swerved the van off the side of the road and back on the highway. The next exit I pulled off the highway and drove to one of my favorite places, Springfield Lake.

When I got there I got out of the van, went down by the lake, and sat there crying and praying. I asked God why he had not answered my prayers for me. I could pray for others and see God answering them but not in my life. God had rejected my prayers; my husband could not love me the way I needed. I don't know how long I stayed there but I knew it had been a long time so I headed home.

Somehow during that time, I had regained strength. God had given me strength to go forward with all that needed to be done.

I returned home and got all the paperwork complete for my divorce. I was too afraid to go to sleep that night for fear of waking up with him beside my bed again. I spent the night on the computer watching out the window all night. Arnold drove by a couple of times and one time he parked in front of the house. I just sat there motionless watching and waiting for him to get out of the car. I kept the phone in my hand as I watched the car. I was going to call the police if he even stepped out of the car toward the house. After about an hour he drove away. I wondered what he must have been thinking about while he was sitting in the car. Was he sorry for what had happened or was he contemplating how to get me back?

The next morning I gathered all the paperwork and took it to my attorney. I was ready to move forward. The thought of the divorce was a weight off my mind as I handed all the completed paperwork to my attorney and explained where Arnold could be served with the petition. My attorney advised me that he would be served sometime that day or the next and to make sure I was safe.

Joanna

CHAPTER 5

I had learned about the Internet, the
dating sites and the way to chat with other
people. Arnold and I had toyed around on the
Internet and we found some sex sites. I knew
that was wrong but I wanted something that
would help our marriage and if sex was it then I
was a willing participant. I know now that
because of our toying on the sex sites and
chatting sex talk caused him to have questions
of my faithfulness to him. Although we never
met these people in person and they were in
other states it was still wrong. After he was gone
from my home, I stayed away from those sites.

I did however want to find a man who could love me more than he ever did. So my search was on. I spent every night on the Internet so that I did not have to go to sleep and every day I was looking for a new job. I made an appointment with a psychologist and since we had taken Craig to a psychologist, I knew just where to go. I soon found out that the psychologist that Craig had gone to had moved to California. But since this was the same firm I made the appointment and was able to get in the next day. After I met with the psychologist, he advised me to go to my family doctor. I called her since she knew me she asked me to come straight in. I went to her and she prescribed me some antidepressants and some sleeping pills. I knew the moment she prescribed them that I was not going to take them. There was no way that I would sleep.

Some of my family was planning to come up the next weekend so I was trying to prepare for them to stay with me. I decided to take the medications the doctor prescribed me so that I could get some sleep.

Some time during the night I woke up feeling the need to breath but not able to get a breath. I realized that something was on my face pressing down hard. I began kicking and trying to scream. The grip on my face was hard. Was I still dreaming? What was happening? I tried to roll over to my stomach but the force of the pillow against my face was more than I could wrestle against. I kept fighting this force whether it was real or a nightmare I still did not know at this point. However I knew I had to get free of the grip.

I reached around and found a face and at that moment I realized someone was trying to kill me. I felt glasses and grabbed them trying to rip them off this person's face. The moment I found the glasses I realized who was trying to kill me. Arnold was trying to kill me. He released the grip on my face and I was able to roll out from under his hand.

I ran downstairs and was able to find the telephone in the dark. I again called 9-1-1. The police were there within minutes. I did not know if he was in the house still or whether he fled out the back door. I just knew I was afraid. When the police arrived I went outside and the police went through the house not finding anyone other than the sleeping kids.

The police asked me if I saw who had done that to me. I had to answer that I never got a good look at him but I knew it was Arnold. They said they could not go after him since I was not sure it was him. I told them that I was sure it was him and they advised me that since I did not actually 'see' him that I could not be sure it was him. They advised me to change the locks on the doors since there was no sign of forced entry. They did say they would protect me from him coming back again, as they would drive by my house at regular intervals.

I didn't take any more of those sleeping (killing) pills as I knew that if I slept the possibility of my not waking up alive was a sure thing after that point. So I just stayed up all night on the Internet. Some nights I would wake up with my head on the keyboard having slept a couple of hours.

That weekend my parents and grandparents got a motel and my brother and sister n law stayed with me. I felt safe with my brother in the house so I slept in my bed for the first time in over a week.

The next morning my sister n law had cooked breakfast and my brother knocked on my bedroom door to tell me that breakfast was ready. I got up and went downstairs and my brother started to tell me that divorce was not the answer that all things could be worked out.

He used the verses in Ecc. 4:9 "Two are better than one; because they have a good reward for their labor". He said God had used Arnold and I together as a team to fulfil God's great work. I could not tell my brother what had happened in our home.

I only told him he did not know the entire story and that I believed God was telling me it was all right to do what I had to do. We began screaming at each other about this, but I still could not tell him all the things I believe now I should have. I went upstairs and got dressed.

My sister n law was crying the kids were crying and my brother was just shaking his head. He told me he didn't know me anymore. I said well too bad there are things you don't know and it's not my place to tell you.

With that I left. As I was walking out the door the kids were asking me 'what about Trish' . . . I said she will be ok "when will you be back?" "I don't know, I just know I have to leave right now" . . . My brother said, "Your making a big mistake!" "Well maybe so but I have to leave" . . . That was about 9:00 in the morning.

I drove south to my favorite place on the planet where I could think, before I got there I decided I needed to calm down so I bought a six pack of beer.

I drove to the lake, put my keys in the glove box, and sat on the back of the van with the back lifted up. I drank those beers as quickly as I could to ease the pain I was feeling inside.

It began to rain and I was feeling loopy not being a drinker it hit me hard. I reached up to close the door on the van and as it was closing I realized that there was no handle on the inside to open it back up again so I just lay there in the back and fell asleep.

When I woke up it was dark outside and I felt like I needed to throw up. I climbed over the seat and opened the van door, the rain still falling and released all the alcohol in my system. I remembered what a tiff I left the house in so I hurried up to go back home.

When I got home Robert was the only one there. He asked if I was ok. I said, "I will be" . . . and went to my room. Robert followed me to my room and told me that Trish was with dad.

I said good I'm glad she is safe. I could not think, I couldn't feel I was just moving with the motions that I knew were there but I still held in everything that was inside of me. Robert told me I needed to talk to him or someone.

We went out to the back deck and he asked me if I was cheating on his dad. I said, "what do you think?" He said, "I don't know but dad says he has proof that you are cheating on him, so are you?" I still would not answer him.

I wanted my kids to know me better than that, better than to believe what their dad would say about me. Robert said there must be some reason that I was so bent on the divorce and if I were cheating it would come out one way or another.

I told him that it was not his business and that God WILL reveal in time what really happened but it was not my place at that time to expose the true problems and definitely not with my children. I wanted them to love their dad as their dad and to trust me as their mom. It was not my place to put my kids in the middle of this mess.

Joanna

CHAPTER 6

The next day Arnold would not let Trish come home, he said I had abandoned her and that I did not deserve to raise her. I tried to talk to my mom and dad but they only believed I had been with a man somewhere. I said I just had to get away and that I was not with anyone.

They would not believe it. They said I was wrong in what I was doing and that I needed to grow up and quit acting like I was sixteen again. That I needed to stop the divorce and get back with Arnold. I advised her that I couldn't do that.

My mom told me that she had suggested he could get a good lawyer and take the kids from me that I was in no shape to finish raising the kids. She said she would not and could not allow Trish to come home with me.

I told her that I had a restraining order against Arnold and the kids were in my custody that he had to allow me to have Trish back. I told her she had no business getting in the middle of it, much less taking the other side and rising against me when she didn't have any of the details of what was going on.

I hung up on her and called the police. I advised the police that they were keeping my daughter without my consent and that I had custody per the restraining order.

The police said they would go get her from the motel room and would be back with her soon. They returned and said that she would be back within the hour. I can't remember how she came home but seeing her was pure bliss to me.

I continued to stay up nights after that for fear of sleep. The next week after the incident I was sitting on the back deck when John came out and said he was leaving. What? Why now? How can you leave me when I need you so much right now? "I'm going to go live with grandma in Oklahoma because I can't deal with this any more. Grandma thinks it will be the best solution for us all."

"What do you mean, you are in your senior year you can't just leave me"

"Yes I have to, I promise I will finish my senior year in Oklahoma, it will be a lot better being out of this situation."

"No, you are my rock, you can't leave."

"Mom, you have problems and I am your son, I need a mom right now and you are not my mom."

I said, "neither is grandma, she is my mom not yours"

John informed me that it had already been worked out and he would be leaving that next week. He apologized for his leaving me but informed me it had to be done. He asked me the same question I had been asked several times already . . .

"Who is it that you have been having an affair with? I know you have because you're not denying it" . . .

I said, "you really believe that don't you?"

He said, "yes, just look at the way your acting" . . .

I said, "well believe what you want, like it would matter anyway, you're leaving!"

Robert came out some time later,

"Are you leaving too?" he answered reassuringly, "No, just John" . . .

"Okay" that was all I could say.

I could not talk about it any more so I went back in the house and straight to the computer where I lived most of my time. I had been chatting with several people on yahoo messenger by that point and decided it was time to start going out I had been asked out several times and one time made a date at an Oyster bar but I stood him up. I knew I needed to get off the computer and make a life.

My mom called sometime after the conversation with John and she advised me that both John and Robert were moving to Oklahoma to live with her and finish their senior year.

"But you are not their mom, how can you act like you are? How can you pretend like that, go behind my back, and ask them to come down there? How dare you?!"

By the end of the week, John was packing his car. Robert had finally confessed that he was leaving too and that I had some psychological problems that needed to be dealt with.

I told him I was trying to deal with them. I was seeing a psychologist 3 times a week. I had not told anyone that I was actually receiving therapy to deal with this.

It did not seem to be helping anything. People still were not asking the right questions and I probably would not have told them anyway.

The next meeting with my therapist was to be the last.

I went in as usual and explained to my therapist that I not only lost my marriage but I also lost my two oldest boys. I was virtually alone in the world. He asked me if I were replacing my husband with the two oldest boys. I didn't think I was but maybe I was, they always seemed so strong they were my stability.

Craig wasn't around much as he found other ways to escape the hell we were in at this point.

Trish needed attention that I could not give her.

I was lost in myself, I could not reach out, I could not fight and I could not talk to anyone.

All I managed to do was sit at the computer and escape into a world that only I knew. I told my therapist that I had been chatting with some men on the Internet and wanted to meet them. He asked me why I wouldn't I said I was afraid.

He told me that I needed to get out and maybe have sex a few times to 'get it out of my system' . . . what?

What was he saying? To give up my moral beliefs and just hop in the sack with any old man who would take me? Why not? It would help you to feel better about yourself, he told me. No, I could not do that – I would not throw away my values to jump in the sack with someone.

Then he said the forbidden – "why not you and I just 'do it' now?"

"Are you kidding?" I snapped at him.

"I could have your license, you are no therapist you are a fake, a fraud, a loser! Geeze! I better never see a bill from you, you slime!"

With that I slammed the door behind me as I walked out of his office.

CHAPTER 7

I got home just as the boys were finishing packing the car for their move to Oklahoma City.

They gave me a hug as they walked past me I tried to convince them one last time that this was not how it should be. We could work it out. I would try to be there for them.

They just told me this was for the best and they hoped I would get some help. I stood in the doorway as I watched them get into the car, back out of the driveway and drive down the street.

I waved and waved and the tears started again. I could not stop them I sobbed as if they both had died. How was I to go on with my life gone?

I gave them everything, I gave up my youth to be their mom and there they go driving down the road to leave me. I was not ready to let them go too.

I could not bear the thoughts that went through my head; I could not eat as every time I tried I threw it up. It was like cancer was in my body and I was fading fast. Now my boys are gone. My babies that I held that I nurtured that I loved with all my heart. How was I to go on? There was nothing I could do to bring them back now.

The next week we were to have the hearing for the restraining order. I was not ready for that. However, I knew I still had business to tend to.

I called a woman at the abuse shelter to stand with me at court as I had no idea what Arnold would try at Court.

Strangely enough when I saw him he tried to smooze me he came over by me and said why are you doing this to me, you know I never have done anything to you. You know I love you and would do anything for you not against you.

What are you thinking? The judge will never grant you this order and you know it. "What?"

Was he living a dream or was his agenda to try to make me look like an idiot. I do not know but every bit of what was said was true and he knew it.

"Respondent, approach the bench" the words came from the Judge as we walked up to the podiums set up in front of the Judge's bench.

"The Petitioner has brought a charge against you stating that you have physically abused her by hitting, kicking, and trying to drown her. How do you plead?"

"I plead, Not guilty your honor." Arnold said.

"So you are standing before me under oath Mr. Arnold stating that Mrs. Arnold is telling less than the truth, is that true?"

"Yes your honor."

Oh my gosh I could not believe he was standing in a courtroom still lying about what had happened. How dare he? Who does he think he is? He treats me like crap and can just stand there with his arrogant self-stating to an officer of the court that I was lying about why we need the restraining order.

"Mrs. Arnold" the Judge addressed me then, "Could you state to this court when and where these incidents took place."

"Yes your honor, it was at our home on Broadway in Springfield Missouri and numerous different occasions, which one would you like me to address first."

"No need Mrs. Arnold, you are stating to this court that Mr. Arnold has brought physical harm to yourself."

"Yes your honor I am"

"Mr. Arnold could you please tell this court that you have always upheld this woman with the utmost respect and decency that a woman you call your wife deserves to be treated?"

"Well, your honor, when a woman deserves to be treated with respect I will treat her with respect." Was Arnold's answer.

"So, you are standing in my courtroom that your wife does not deserve to be treated with respect?"

"I guess I am your honor"

I stood there as if everything were in slow motion I had hoped that for my sake he would just admit to hurting me. I would have liked for once in his life he would admit to the pain that he caused me but no.

He stood there and outright lied to the court telling them he never hurt me and that I did not deserve to be treated with respect.

"In light of your own testimony Mr. Arnold I will have to grant the Stay against you. Do you understand what that means?"

"Yes" he said "yes I do"

"Well it means Mr. Arnold that you are to have no communication with Mrs. Arnold, you are not to disturb her, you are not to be within 50 yards of her home, you are not to call her on the phone you are to stay away from her at all times. The matter of your children, Mrs. Arnold, has your husband ever taken a hand against his children?"

"Your honor Mr. Arnold has been a good father to our daughter. He has had some blow ups with the boys but they have worked those issues out."

"Well Mrs. Arnold I cannot grant visitation since we do have a pending divorce but for the meantime I will grant custody with you and liberal visitation with Mr. Arnold, is that acceptable? Mr. Arnold you will pick your daughter up from school on the days you both can agree to have her and you will drop her off in front of your house when you return her."

Joanna

CHAPTER 8

I had gone into that courtroom thinking that I would be vindicated instead, I felt sad. Sad that it had come to this, sad that I knew Arnold would not be able to admit the truth. I felt sad that we could not work through the problems from the very beginning. Sad that I did not have my husband and two oldest boys waiting for me when I got home.

Then I was mad, mad at God for allowing all this to happen, mad that he had taken the one man that was always able to stop the violence in our home, Eddis, mad that God wouldn't answer my prayers to change my husband. I was so mad I could not see straight. I went to my car and just sat there for a while. I could not drive in the state I was in at that time, I had a hard time even walking to my car.

The emptiness inside my soul was so big a freight train could have driven inside and there would still be room for more. Why had my life come to this?

The next morning I received a visitor, a preacher friend Arnold and I relied upon, a friend who had been there with us and sat down with us when we were having problems with our teenage sons. He had helped us in a way he will never know and we loved him for loving us and for praying for us. I was excited to see him at the door with my pastor.

Finally, I can share some of my story. I hugged their necks and asked them to come in and have a seat and offered them something to drink.

The first thing said to me was, "Joanna you know we love you." The voice trailed off.

Oh no I have to turn back to my defenses. I will not be able to share my story because they already have their own ideas about what was going on. I knew at that point that I would not be able to tell either one of them anything. I must revert to survival mode.

God already knows so why do I have to continue to defend what decision I have made.

He continued with his statement, "We know you have had affairs, and are trying to hurt Arnold, we don't know why the devil has entered you and why you have allowed it. We cannot allow you to bring a man of God down with you. The restraining order was just a ploy to trap Arnold and we cannot stand by and watch you hurt a man who has done nothing but try to serve God.

You must confess your alcoholism and drug addiction and your addiction to sex in front of the church so that we can pray with you and help you with your problems."

"What affairs, what alcoholism, what sex addiction, I'm not doing any of that!"

I tried to tell them and I was told that I didn't have to hide it any longer that God already knew my sin and all I needed to do was confess and I would be restored to the fold. What the heck and what right did they have to come into my home accusing me of such idiocies? What poison had they been fed by the man I called my husband for 18 years?

"I'm not going before anyone to admit to something I never did!" I said to both of them.

"Well in that case we are going to have to ask you not to come back to our church, you are not welcome there until you are willing to confess your sins before men, we have done what we can, you are in the hands of an angry God." Sternly the words came from his mouth.

I asked them both to leave, I told them I appreciated their concern but they had the story wrong. They left and I just sat there numb.

I couldn't believe what I was hearing how could men of God, men I had trusted, men that had been in our home whom I had prayed with. How could they believe such lies about me?

I knew God wanted to use me up until then but if I was not welcome in the church then I must find somewhere I could worship.

I had been chatting with a man who seemed like a good man. His name was Mark. He had invited me to attend his worship service that he sang in the church and was singing a special that next Sunday so I decided to go.

I attended the Southland Christian Church and felt the power of God there the minute I walked into the sanctuary. I loved it, I could not stop crying the tears flowed like Niagara Falls but they were tears of joy tears that I was actually in the House of God. They passed the bread and I did not feel worthy to take of the communion so I only passed it on.

A lady standing down from me came over by me and put her arm around me and prayed for me. Her name was Becky. What a feeling to hear someone pray for me.

It had been a long time the last person I had heard pray aloud for me without criticism was Bro. Eddis. After the service I went up to Mark and told him how much his song meant to me. He could not believe I actually came to church. He hugged me and told me to return that night for a fellowship the church was having.

Mark became a very good friend from the first time I met him and he was to remain a friend through many more hard times in my life. We both had just decided to begin dating again and he was dating and encouraged me to go ahead and meet some of the men on the Internet and go out with them. Therefore, he became my security call when I would go out.

I decided that week to go ahead and set up some dates with some of the men I had met on the Internet. I would meet them at a park in the city and before I left I would call Mark and give him as much information as I could and tell him where I was going.

The first man I met was named Bobby, he seemed like a nice man, and he worked for the Assembly of God Church. I met him at the park and we left there and drove around just talking.

I met him two more times after that and found out that he was married. What the heck? I did not know Christian men did that. I felt as if I had betrayed his wife. It was wrong. I could not see him nor talk to him again.

I continued to meet some of the men that I had been chatting with and was having a great time. Most of them treated me great. I was given flowers by one man and was going out to the theater and live plays. I was having the time of my life. I was feeling much better than I had in a long time.

However, something inside was missing. I still felt empty. I went to the park to meet one man and he was sitting at the table when I walked up and he had Taco Bell sacks sitting on the table. I thought how nice.

"You're not Joanna are you?"

"Yes I am."

I was smiling as I walked toward him.

"So your Bill?"

He then said "I wish I weren't"

I was not sure I heard him correctly, "Excuse me?"

"Well your fat" he told me, like I did not know that already

"Well I guess so but you're rude and your cheap – Taco Bell what were you thinking, I'm going home!"

I drove home and called Mark crying he told me I did the right thing that I did not need to be around anyone like that. He advised me that I wasn't fat I was fluffy and then he just laughed. Which in turn made me laugh too.

He reminded me that there were still jerks out there that would say such stupid things and I did not need them. I felt a lot better then.

Joanna

CHAPTER 9

I had found a good job at a law firm as their receptionist and would also be working some cases and handling all the billing for the firm. I was happy because the severance pay was just about used up.

Scott the attorney who hired me told me that my family came first and if I ever needed to take care of anything with the divorce or with my daughter then he would completely work with me.

I knew I found a good job. He told me that my last job gave me a glowing reference so I was pleased that they had kept their word.

I still was afraid to sleep at night and it had been almost a month. The most sleep I got was when I would fall asleep at the computer chatting with people. I was constantly tired and my boss told me that I should take a nap on the sofa in the conference room.

Most days I took him up on it and asked him if he would make sure I was awake when lunch was over. Most of the time I was only able to sleep about 30 minutes. Scott had told me that I probably needed to get into a divorce support group.

I went to one but it was gross watching the men googoo over the pretty women and ignore that I was there so I never went back.

Thirty days had gone by and we had not received an answer from Arnold on the divorce so we went to Court to finalize it. I was elated that he had not followed through and hired an attorney. This was going to be an easy divorce after all.

I had not even told Arnold that we were going to court that day. I drove up to the courthouse and thought I saw Arnold's car, maybe it was my imagination I thought.

I walked into the courthouse and he was sitting there with this woman. I knew her to be a well-known attorney in Springfield with a reputation that proceeded her. She was a wolf, a complete wolf.

She would eat me alive.

I began searching for my attorney and could not find him. Then I saw him. "Jason" I said as I saw him. "I know I know they filed their answer yesterday and the divorce will not go on". What?

He told me that we could file an objection but the Judge usually granted filing out of time for any reason, he deems necessary. When we went into the courtroom Arnold was sitting across the isle from me.

He said, "I bet you didn't expect to see me here" I could not talk to him I did not want to look at him. I tried to stay calm but inside I felt as if I could not breathe, I thought I was going to pass out right there in the courtroom. My attorney was called up before the Judge.

He explained to the Judge that the thirty days had run but the wolf interrupted him and advised they had a motion to file out of time due to the fact that I had threatened her client and he decided to seek legal counsel. What? Threatened HIM? That was absurd!

She then went on to tell the Judge that I was having men stay the night with me in my home while the minor child was present. I did not remember that happening! What a slime I thought as I stood there shaking. I turned my head and caught Arnold smiling looking straight at me. I felt as if he had won. Won? What? Won what? What was there to win?

Nobody wins in divorce I wanted to shout out right there in the Courtroom. My attorney advised the judge that he had the Decree and it was fair and if he would excuse us to go mediate then we could finalize this today. The wolf said "Under no terms would I be willing to sit in a conference room with that woman who has done nothing but seek to slander this innocent man!" Therefore, the judge dismissed us all. Jason gave her a copy of the Decree and advised her to look it over, it was as fair as it could be.

She had advised my attorney as we were walking out of the courtroom that I was an unfit mother and they would have my daughter. She also advised him that the two oldest boys had been emancipated (declared legal adults) and were making their own living in Oklahoma.

She advised him that my younger son was a runaway and was no longer living in the home because the three older boys could not stay in the same home with the likes of me. I left that courthouse feeling defeated!

CHAPTER 10

I got home and my phone was ringing. It was Mark; he had called hoping that I was free. I began telling him everything that happened I told him that Arnold's attorney was telling vicious lies about me and I did not understand why that was happening. He would have to stop me because he could not understand me since I could not stop crying. He asked me to meet him at McGuffee's Restaurant so we could talk that evening. I met him there and then went to church, as he wanted me to get into the choir with him. I enjoyed my church and was feeling closer to God again.

Days turned into weeks and I continued to date. I met some great men and found some great friends with whom I could talk to.

I made some mistakes during that time in my choices of whom I was dating. Never did I did not want to be locked down to one man. I wanted to be free. I was enjoying my life free.

Most days I would come home from work to find my answering machine full of messages most from Arnold. He begged me to let him come home. He spent a lot of time reminding me that I was going against God and that if I had remained submissive to him then my life would have been a lot better.

He would be passionate and caring almost convincing me that it would be good again. I would not fall for it. It had taken me too long to get where I was. I felt as if I were alone in the world and had lost all of my family and friends, however I was free of the horrible nightmares that I had lived with.

I did not want to have that happen to me ever again, so I continued my lookout every night as I typed words to people on the Internet. Most every night at least twice Arnold would drive by and park the car a few houses down from the house and he would just sit in his car. I often wondered what he must be thinking as he sat there.

Was he truly sorry for what he had lost or did he feel vindicated for what he had brought me to? I could not let him know he had brought me to this level in my life. I could not let him know he had won.

It is true that nobody wins in divorce; we were all losers, everyone in my family. My children had lost their mom to the Internet and deep inside herself. They had also lost their dad, as his life was not what they had remembered. My parents had lost their daughter to a world they could not understand, our friends had lost both of us as we had been taught so many times that a married couple should not be friends with the single community. Our Sunday school class had lost a teacher who loved each one of them as much as she loved her own children.

We were all losers true! Inside I still felt as if Arnold had won. He had taken my sanity, he took my church, he took my family, and he ran my kids away from me. He had won!

I could find nobody who knew me before that would listen to my side of the story without criticisms and condemnation. I felt and truly believed in my heart that nobody cared about me, I felt no prayers being said for me, and felt as if nobody would care if I dropped off the face of the earth.

I had already tried the suicide thing and I could not do that mainly for the sake of my children. I was lost, and only sunk deeper inside myself and this altered reality that I had created on the Internet and with people who did not know me. I felt safe there, I wouldn't ruin Arnold and he could go on preaching as he wanted to and I would not be blamed for his not preaching.

CHAPTER 11

I tried not to blame Arnold and I tried to remember that I had made my choices in life and the outcome would be up to me. I would be the undoing of myself and nobody would be the blame for it. I was so lost in myself that the next months were a blur.

I had little recognition of which I was any longer. I had sunk into deep despair and depression toppled with sleep deprivation. Trish spent every Wednesday night and Friday night with her dad and she seemed to be enjoying the time with her father. Sometimes she would stay Saturday night with him and go to church with him. Most Saturday nights she stayed home and went to church with me.

We were going to church at Southland Christian Church where I had finally been able to become active again in the Choir and was enjoying my Sunday School class. One Saturday night Trish told me that she wanted to go to her dad's apartment that next day after church and stay the night with him on Sunday.

I told her that I had no problem with that and encouraged her to spend time with her dad. We went to church Sunday morning and Mark reminded us that Sunday afternoon there was going to be an all church skating party at the skating rink.

I asked Trish if she wanted to go or if she wanted to meet her dad. I told her that she needed to call her dad to let him know we would be later than expected and not to wait on her.

She said, "He will be okay."

I told her that she really needed to call him that he was going to be mad if she did not. She said she would deal with dad that she did not really want to call him right then. I did not think about it again as we went to eat lunch with Mark and meet the rest of the church members at the skating rink. We had such a good time and were laughing about the fun time we had at the skating rink.

We got home and I saw a note on the door from Arnold he was not happy and you could tell it in the note. Trish said, "Oh, he will be all right." So we wadded up the note and threw it in the trash.

I went upstairs and called a friend of mine and was talking to him on the phone when I heard Arnold yelling at Trish downstairs.

I went to the top of the stairs, still on the phone; Arnold began yelling at me telling me that I was ruining his entire life and that I had turned Trish against him. He was angry and yelling and telling me that I would pay for my actions of making him worry about his daughter all day.

My friend told me to hang up the phone and call 911 that Arnold was breaking the restraining order by being in the house.

Before I could do anything, Arnold had ran up to the head of the stairs where I was standing and he grabbed the phone out of my hand. I began screaming downstairs to Trish telling her to call 911.

Arnold was backing me into the wall asking me who I was talking to, "Is that the guy you were sleeping with while we were married?"

"No, but if you want to think I was cheating on you during the time we were married Okay then, yes and it was great" I don't even know why I answered anything. I was so angry that he would not let go of the cheating thing.

He was pushed up against me yelling in my face, "I knew you were cheating, I just had to hear you admit it." Yeah, okay well, will you let me go then? I thought as my neck was hurting from his arm being bent into my throat holding me against the wall.

"Trisha is calling 911 and the police will be here any time".

"She won't call 911 she knows I'm right, you are worthless".

He pushed me on the bed I was able to stand back up and I kicked him in the shin.

I started to run out of the room when he grabbed my arm and pulled me around to the top of the stairs and said, "I can push you down these stairs right now and say you fell."

I said, "You would do that right in front of your daughter?"

About that time I looked down and saw Trish standing at the foot of the stairs, "Stop dad, you're hurting her."

"I'm not hurting anybody, your mom is just making a lot of noise." He said to her.

"Well I called 911 and the lady wants to talk to you."

"Look! You poisoned her against me!" He yelled at me as he let go and ran down the stairs.

As he ran out of the house, he pushed Trish out of the way. He peeled out of the driveway and down the street. Trish and I were both standing there holding each other while I was trying to talk to the 9-1-1 dispatcher when the police arrived.

There were four cars that pulled up at once. Trish and I walked outside before they got to the door. One of the officers asked if we were all right. We both said we were. Another officer asked where he went. I told him that he probably went to the church. I told him where it was and reminded him that the Sunday night services were about to start but they could probably find him by the bus barn just north of the church building. Two of the police cars left to go that way.

One of the police officers asked me if he could talk to Trish in private. I said sure. They went in the living room and I could see him talking to her. I stood outside talking to another officer.

Someone called on his walkie-talkie that they had the subject in custody.

"Does he have to go to jail?" I didn't want him to go to jail, I wanted him to be the husband that I had seen in him before, I wanted him to love me, I didn't want any more strife in our home, I wanted peace!

The officer that was talking to Trish came outside with us.

"Mrs. Arnold he is going to jail and you can't stop this from happening. I realize you are afraid of what he will do when he gets out but we will continue to drive by your house at night and make sure he doesn't try anything else."

I had watched a police car drive by every night since filing the first police report. I do not know how many times, but why had not they done something when he was parked down the street? I assume they did not find him to be a threat just sitting in his car.

CHAPTER 12

The next day I went to work, after I got home a couple who had been our close friends from college and church showed up at my door.

Again, I was so happy to see some friends from church. "Come on in, have a seat, would you like some tea, I made a cheesecake would you like a piece"?

"No thank you, we just came by to let you know that pastor bailed Arnold out of jail today."

Fear overcame me and I did not know what to say. Were they here to warn me or to advise me? Should I find a place to hide out for a few days, had Arnold told them he was going to make me pay for what had happened?

"Joanna" my friend said in a low slow voice, "We just want to know why you would make up such lies about the man you love, the man who has done nothing but good for you, a man who loves God with all his heart"? He continued, "This man is hurting and you had to trap him by asking him to come over so you could call the police and have them come and put handcuffs on him right in front of the church where everyone could see". "We just want to know what your agenda is."

I could not believe I was hearing what I was hearing could these people really be my friends? How could they come with straight accusations without even hearing my side of it? How could anyone just sit on my couch and begin a conversation in this way?

I did not know what to say. I honestly did not know what to say and I just wanted them to leave right then. I did not want to try to defend my stance on this situation.

My friends were sitting there expecting me to respond they both just sat there looking at me.

"Do you have anything to say?" One of them finally asked me.

"Well" . . . I paused still not knowing what to say as I continued, "sometimes things aren't exactly what they seem."

"Yeah, you're not what you seem. We know you have been drinking and staying up all hours on the Internet. We know you've been meeting lots of men, we know that the Christian testimony you tried to show us is a complete fraud. Should I go on about what else we know about you?"

"Well it looks like you already have your mind made up so I guess I have nothing more to add to it." Why could I not just tell them exactly what went on in that house? Why could I not just scream out that he was a fraud? "I just have one thing to say, Arnold is not innocent in all this he and I both went out drinking before we split up, we both were looking at sex sites on the internet, and Arnold has not always been nice to me."

Okay I started a dialogue. I tried to show them that the picture that Arnold painted of himself was not an accurate portrayal. Maybe now they can ask the right questions so I can tell them more about what really has been happening in our home. I was wrong.

"How can you continue to tell all these lies, no wonder you don't sleep at night, a person with many lies inside their soul does not sleep." With that he got up and took his wife's hand. "I can't believe we called you our friend!"

No, that was my line, you can't tell me that when you didn't even come over to find out how I was or if there was anything I needed, no you just come over expecting an apology for something I did not do. It was not going to happen. If they did not want an explanation then why would they even waste their time coming by? I did not understand it.

CHAPTER 13

I was living in a fog and I knew that fogs always lifted, I waited for the fog to lift but it seemed that more fog continued to creep in. I could not close the door on it, I could not escape it, and I could only live it. It was cold and lonely in my world.

It seemed that my old friends and family had left me and so many people were against me. John and Robert had escaped this hell that was still going on. They would not talk to me. I tried to call them and my mom would just remind me that the boys did not want to talk to me. I was not their mom anymore. I had caused too much hurt in their lives and I needed to admit to them and to her that I just did not care about them or what was happening in their lives.

My mom had told me that the boys were playing football again and it was pretty sorry of me that I not even try to attend one of their games. I didn't have the money to take a trip for the weekend, it wasn't that I didn't care because I did and the pain of my boys leaving me and not wanting anything more to do with me hurt worse than death itself. I can understand why the boys left but escaping is not the answer.

They should have not run away from the problems, they should have stayed; the problems in their lives did not go away just because they left. The rest of us did not get to get away from the situation and their leaving only caused more problems for them. The anger and bitterness they were holding inside could not have been good for them.

My mom told me that Arnold was sending the boys money sometimes and it would be helpful if I were to send money.

I was not the one who suggested John and Robert leave, and besides I am struggling just to pay the bills as it were. I tried to explain to my mom. Why could no one understand?

"No, Joanna, this is your doing and you can stop it anytime you want to. Just stop the silliness and get your heart right with God and stop the divorce and get back together. God will take care of things."

"Mom, I can't do that, and besides who are you or anyone to tell me where my heart is with God? I can't live like that anymore."

"Joanna, you know I think you have exaggerated things. I think for your own sanity you should learn to forgive and just get back together."

"Mom, you saw Arnold in his rages, you know how he has gotten, and you watched him try to kill Craig in our front yard. How can you sit there and tell me that it is better that I live in hell? You remember the time I went with dad to my uncle's funeral and even dad told me I needed to get out of there for my own safety."

"Well Joanna, you know that happens to Arnold when he doesn't get enough sleep or when you guys are under a lot of stress, otherwise he is a great husband."

"I know mom but since Bro. Eddis died, Arnold's rages were too much and I just could not deal with it anymore. There is nobody here that can look at things objectively."

My mom continued, "Maybe you should look at yourself and try to see what you had done wrong, maybe you aren't walking close enough to God to know what He is trying to tell you. Maybe you are drinking too much to have a clear mind about the issues."

"Mom, yes I did drink one time but that was it." It was doing me no good to continue to have these conversations with my mom. She had her ideas of what was happening because Arnold had convinced her that I was the one who was breaking up the marriage. Yes I was to some extent but he was the reason I was and he failed to mention that point. I tried to see what I had done to cause this and I honestly could not see what I could have done differently.

CHAPTER 14

It was better for me to just make new friends and try to realize that my old friends and my entire family except for Craig and Trish were dead to me.

If anyone had spoke to Arnold before me or heard through the grapevine that I needed a lot of prayer they seemed unwilling to talk to me. Most just wanted to accuse me, or tell me that they were praying for me. Good I needed a lot of prayer but somehow I felt it were only words, as God was not taking me out of any of this situation. He was not making it better nor was he giving me any peace.

Therefore, I continued meeting new people who did not know me before the divorce. It was easier that way. They could make their own conclusions about me

I had been chatting with a man and his wife on the Internet and they invited me to come down for Karaoke at a local bar. I decided to go one weekend and meet them.

It would be a nice change from the alternative. I walked in the smoke filled bar and ordered the strongest drink I could think of a Hurricane. It was a Friday night and Trish was with her dad. I drank the first Hurricane so fast it made the tips of my fingers tingle.

We laughed and were having so much fun making fun of all the singers. Then one of the people at the table asked me if I could sing. I said I could try so I went up to the stage and looked at the songs they had.

I did not recognize any of them by name so my newly found friend came up and she suggested a song. It was easy since the words were on the screen so I began to sing. It was amazing; the crowd would not let me get down. I had not had that much fun in so long. The people loved me singing.

After the third Hurricane, I decided it was time for me to get off the stage. I tripped over the microphone and fell off the stage. I was mortified and definitely drunk.

I hated that feeling but it was nice because it overshadowed the fear and depression I had felt for so long before that. I was afraid to drive home knowing how drunk I was so my new friends offered to drive me home.

I rode with the wife while she drove my van to my house and her husband followed us. I thanked them for the night and went into the dark cold lonely house.

I remembered that I was alone in this world. I was so alone and so . . . Oh I was so drunk.

I tried to climb the stairs to get to my bedroom and kept tripping on the bottom stair so I sat on the sofa for a minute.

I needed to go the bathroom but it was upstairs so I decided that if I crawled up the stairs maybe I could make it.

I woke up sometime later lying on the floor in the hall not having made it to the bathroom or to my bedroom. I was so tired but I cleaned up the mess and went to bed not afraid for the first time in a long time.

Joanna

CHAPTER 15

The holidays of 1999 were fast approaching, as it had been almost four months since I had thrown Arnold out after the first main fight.

My days were long and the nights were even longer as I continued the watchful eye out the window of the computer room during the week.

I looked forward to Friday nights as sometime during that time I had figured out that when I was drunk I felt nothing. Every sense was dulled I did not cry, nor did I feel any emotion. I was not scared any more when I was drinking and I felt safe when Trish was with her dad.

I did not think he would try anything while she was with him. So I used the time to drink and I was drinking a lot during that time.

I was still going to church and did feel guilty when I was at church even though I had stooped to such a low place in my life.

I tried to find God somewhere but no matter where I turned, it felt as if He had closed the door on me. He had not fixed things like I thought he promised and he had not brought my boys back and I was not finding true peace.

Things had calmed down between Arnold and I and the blow-ups were fewer. Maybe spending a night in jail helped. I began to wonder if he really could change. I had hoped that for someone else's sake because I did not want him back in my life.

My life was becoming quiet with less drama. I asked Arnold if we could have this divorce finished by the New Year so that we could both go on with our lives. He told me it depended on me since I would not allow the courts to say John and Robert were emancipated. They were not supporting themselves, because my parents were supporting them, and there was no court order stating they were emancipated. I believed they were just running when they should have stayed with me.

One night Arnold came over to the house and we went through all the home videos together and separated all the videos and pictures and we actually had a good time doing that.

We laughed and we cried together as we watched a lot of them to decide who took which ones. We watched the videos of camp and laughed our heads off.

It made me remember the time that we were driving to camp. We had an old Buick station wagon that I was driving full of kids and Arnold was driving the van full of kids following us.

One of the kids in the back of the station wagon told me to take the next exit so I did. We were laughing so hard as we got back on the highway with Arnold following us in the van.

The next exit came and we did it again, as we exited the highway a second time only to return to the highway yet again we were all laughing so hard I was having a hard time driving. The kids and I were having a blast when I saw Arnold speed the van up next to me and it was evident on his face he was not a happy camper.

He motioned for me to pull off at the next service station that I had put the kids in danger. I knew I was in big trouble.

The kids all went into the store laughing about what we just did as Arnold came over to my side of the car with his hand in my side as hard as he could push and began telling me to grow up and quit being stupid.

He said that if we I did not want a fight in front of the kids I would do as I was told. That must have been a couple of years before as I sat there in my living room watching those videos and remembering it as if it were last week. Even then remembering driving off the highway and back on made me chuckle inside. Those kids had no idea how mad Arnold was. It was easy giving up several videos since I did not want too many memories creeping up inside of me. It was more peaceful without the memories haunting me at every corner.

CHAPTER 16

Thanksgiving was always a great time for our family and I was looking forward to going to Oklahoma City to help with the cooking and spend time with the boys, John and Robert.

There had been only a few times they would talk to me on the phone and those calls were short and vague. I was looking forward to actually sitting down with each of them in hopes of restoring our relationships.

I knew they were adjusting well living with their grandparents but inside I felt they forgot that I was still their mother. I was going to take some time to spend with each son and hopefully we could talk about what was happening.

I knew they were hurting inside about the entire situation and they needed to talk to me about how mad they were with me for spending all my time in a world only I could penetrate.

I called my mom and she thought it would be a great idea for me to come down. She informed me that the boys had in fact missed me a lot and they felt as if they had lost their mother.

She told me how they were doing and what was going on in their lives. It was hard to hear about them as it was like I was hearing about my nephews or something and not my own children I did not know what to say.

She told me that Arnold and I could stay with her and the kids would have both of their parents together for the holidays.

NO! I was not going to do that. What do you mean Arnold is staying there? He is not your son and we are getting a divorce! I could not believe I was even hearing this! "Mom, Arnold and I are not getting back together and it is time that the kids realize that we are getting a divorce."

My mom thought she was doing a good thing trying to help Arnold and I work out the problems but there was still so much more that she was unaware of. I still could not tell her everything.

She believed marriage was forever and there was nothing that could break up a marriage short of infidelity and there had been none of that between Arnold and I that I was aware of.

She informed me that Arnold still loved me and he could forgive me for my infidelities. "My infidelities?" I asked her.

"Yes, Arnold loves you no matter what you have done, just like Hosea continued to love his adulteress and drunken wife." What was I hearing, Arnold was the Hosea? I was definitely not Gomer.

"Mom, I am not coming, I'm sorry for the kids but I cannot live a fraudulent life. Arnold and I are getting a divorce and we are no longer a family as you knew it." What more was I to say? All my intentions of spending time with the boys were gone. I would not be a part of their holiday. I could not be thankful for anything at that point. Not when I had lost everything already.

I explained to Craig and Trish that I was not going to go with them for the holidays but if they wanted to spend Thanksgiving with their dad I understood and I thought it was a good idea.

Joanna

I would use that time to paint the living room while they were gone. They did not like the idea of this being the first holiday that they did not spend with mom but they understood. I made Trish promise me that she would call me on Thanksgiving from grandma's house so that I could talk to everyone.

CHAPTER 17

The house was quiet with Trish and Craig both gone. I had time to paint the living room and I found time between to explore and chat more on the Internet. I was invited to Thanksgiving dinner with some members of the church but I did not think it would be a good idea and I felt that I would spoil their atmosphere so I stayed home. I went to the movie store and rented several tear-jerking movies that I wanted to watch by myself.

I had been chatting on the Internet with a man in Northern Missouri and he was also online the night before Thanksgiving. I bore my soul to him and explained that my children were in Oklahoma for the holidays.

He invited me for dinner with him and I volunteered to cook the turkey if he wanted me to come up there. He seemed like a nice man through our chats and I wanted to meet him. On Thursday morning he called me and suggested that he was going to go to his mother's house for Thanksgiving and would not be staying home. I advised him it wouldn't feel right to meet his mother the same day I met him so I declined to go up there.

I painted while watching the movies and would take breaks to go upstairs to chat with anyone who might be online on Thanksgiving Day.

I was terribly lonely when the phone rang. It was Trish calling me from her grandma's house. The sounds coming over the phone was almost more than I could bear; however I kept my emotions in check as the phone was passed from person to person.

I was able to speak with all my children and each conversation was short and cordial. After I hung up the phone I cried for a couple of hours knowing that this was the first Thanksgiving I had ever missed with my family. I felt so alone in the world.

The next day I was on the Internet chatting with different men as usual and one guy I was chatting with asked me to meet him at a local restaurant for dinner, his name was Gary.

I met Gary at a restaurant in town, he was a very tall man 6 foot 7 inches tall and he had never been married. He was about 4 years younger than I was and the conversation at dinner was great.

We left the restaurant and he came to my house to help me finish painting the living room. We had a great time and I do believe we had more paint on ourselves than we did on the wall. However, we were able to complete the entire living room and it looked fresh and clean.

I felt this was a new beginning. We spent most of the rest of the weekend together just having a good time and learning about each other. The weekend was refreshing after all, I was able to sleep every night knowing that I was not in danger.

Joanna

CHAPTER 18

The thoughts inside my head were under control when I was alone. I did not worry about things I felt as if I had no emotions. I knew I did not want to be alone the rest of my life and I was desperate to find someone.

The man I spent Thanksgiving weekend with was a great man however I wanted to be able to meet more men. He and I enjoyed fishing and spending time at the lake. We saw each other about once a week for several weeks. Other nights I would set up two or three dates in one day. I was enjoying the attention I was getting from the men.

Some people had the notion that if you were abused you did not want a man again. That was not the case for me. I wanted to be loved, to feel protected and to know that there was someone out there that could love me more than my husband ever had. So I continued to look for the man for me even if doing so was in the wrong place with the wrong intent.

A couple of weeks passed and my mom called and advised me that they really wanted me to come down to Oklahoma for Christmas. I asked her if Arnold was going to be there. She advised me that he would be and I should be also. I declined to go yet again for another holiday. Since I had made it through Thanksgiving alone I knew it would be hard to be alone again but I knew I could do it.

I went shopping and prepared the presents for John and Robert. I could not buy much since I was having a hard time making the bills stretch. Arnold was not paying any child support because we could not reach a settlement. John and Robert's income was gone and I was making a lot less that I was making at the Telephone Company but I was happy to have a job.

The month between Thanksgiving and Christmas was a blur to me as I blindly walked through the motions. I was going to work and home and straight to the Internet that had consumed my complete being. I was still sharing my story and meeting new people yet something inside was still missing. Most of the men I met on the Internet seemed shallow and did not seem to care too much about what I was going through. There were a few men who became very good friends and a great support.

It was the week before Craig and Trish were to leave to go to Oklahoma for Christmas. Both of them voiced their opinion of leaving me for yet another holiday alone. I assured them I would be all right as I was renting several sappy love story movies and would spend my day watching those. We had Christmas at the house before they left.

The house was dark, empty and lonely, as I would walk through looking for signs of the kids, knowing they were gone. I took time to sit on each of the kid's beds and I prayed for each of them. I missed them around me but more than that I did not know how to get back the relationship with John and Robert. I knew nothing about their lives. They were gone and I was dead to them. I knew they were hurting about the entire mess that had happened yet I still could not talk to them about all the facts, as they did not need to hear the entire story.

I did not want them thinking of their dad as anything other than their dad. It seemed as if John and Robert had forgotten about the hell that we had lived in, as they were completely safe from all of it at their grandmother's house 300 miles away. My fear continued to be that they had run from their problems without facing them head on and this would cause life long trauma for them unless they learned to deal with it.

I would sit at the computer looking at the screen hoping someone would chat with me as I had so many pent up feelings and emotions however only a few people were online and I couldn't get much conversation from any of them. I mostly sat and watched my movies cuddled in a blanket to allow myself the time to cry.

The thoughts inside my head were under control when I was alone. I did not worry about things I felt as if I had no emotions. I knew I did not want to be alone the rest of my life and I was desperate to find someone.

CHAPTER 19

Somehow inside I still felt empty as I continued to go to bars on Friday nights when I didn't have a date or I would even sometimes set up meetings at different bars with my friends I had met at the Karaoke bar. I knew that going to the bars on Friday and then going to church on Sunday seemed like a double standard and I did not feel good about it. I continued to remain friends with Mark from my church and we would pair up when the church had activities. I enjoyed being with Mark but he never indicated he felt anything more than a friendship with me so I left it alone and enjoyed the time we spent together as friends.

I tried to be careful about remaining pure, as I did not want to hop in the sack with anyone. I wanted a meaningful relationship before I decided to go to the next step. I began using my lunch hour to write poetry. I worked about a mile from Springfield Lake and would go to the lake and write and think about things. The words just flowed from the pen as I continued to write poetry about my dreams in life. I wanted to find a man to love me as much as I loved him; I just had no idea that I was going about it the wrong way.

I took the time to watch each movie I had rented for the week the kids would be in Oklahoma for Christmas. I cried a lot and released all of the emotions that I had so carefully held inside. There was nobody there to see the hurt flow as I dreamed about my knight and shiny armor running out to save me. I knew it was just a fantasy but it was my fantasy as I watched 'Hope Floats', 'Sleepless in Seattle', and a number of other movies.

I worked the week between Christmas and New Year on New Year's Eve one of the girls asked me to come out to her place for her New Year's Eve party. I agreed as I thought it would be a good change from sitting at home since that week most of the people I had been dating were busy with family for the holidays.

I arrived at her home with a bottle of some sort of liquor in hand. I saw her kitchen cabinet was full of different types of liquor and there were two kegs of beer. I was not used to seeing that much alcohol in anybody's home it seemed strange to me. I fixed myself a drink and went out on her deck and began talking to several people that were there.

I was enjoying myself as we counted down the clock for the New Year as well as the New Millennium. I believed this would be MY year. I thought in my head that I was starting to gain control of my life even though it was continuing to spiral out of control.

We went outside and began shooting fireworks to bring in the New Year. My head started spinning and I was unable to hold myself up, as I was completely drunk. I walked back into the house and sat on the sofa. I guess I looked pretty bad as my co-worker kept asking me if I was all right. Sometime later I woke up on her floor and a blanket was wrapped around me. I had no idea what happened after I sat down on the sofa. My stomach felt as if rocks had fell to the bottom of it. I was so sick.

As soon as I was able to move I went straight to my van and drove myself home. I was sick the rest of the day. That was the last time I would drink for a long time. I vowed to myself that I had to stop the partying and get it together without the drinking. I could stand up straight and not be afraid without the alcohol. I knew then that God could help me.

Joanna

CHAPTER 20

The day was approaching when it was time to finish the divorce. I had been asked several times if I was going to have a divorce party. No, how could I celebrate a failure? Inside I still had the thoughts that I could have made this work. I could have done something to change him. I could have prayed more. I could have told the 'right' people what was going on in our house. However, the only man that I could ever be completely honest with about our situation was in heaven.

We had already been to court several times and more motions were heard. I was beginning to believe this was not going to happen. Then the day came it was my mother n law's birthday, February 15th, 2000 she would be celebrating today. I saw Arnold in the hallway of the courtroom and my heart sank to the floor. All the emotions pent up inside were struggling to burst out at any time.

I felt a loss like never before in my life. How could a marriage of 18 years just be washed down the toilet with only a hit of the gavel and a signature on a piece of paper? I had loved this man with all my being. I wanted our marriage to last, I wanted to be loved, and I wanted to share the joys of standing next to one another as each of our children gave their hands to another in marriage. I wanted to share our grandchildren together. I wanted to stand next to my husband as he preached the Word of God. I wanted to encourage him in every way possible. I sat there knowing that I could not do any of those things. Our marriage was finished, done, washed up. Satan had won and we had lost everything.

As I walked out of the courtroom I realized we had all lost. I was divorced from Arnold and John and Robert as the Decree stated that John and Robert were emancipated. What a blow!

My children whom I had given up everything to have and raise had divorced me. It made me think of all the things that had happened throughout my life.

My parents were the best parents a kid could ask for. They were not the problem. I was. The first time I had been raped I was six years old. It was horrifying. I fought and was held down by my hair. I remember asking the person who was lying on top of me what he was doing and he just told me to be quiet or someone would hear me. So I remained quiet. I learned at too early of an age that if you give in then the men cannot take anything from you. You are a willing participant and they will not hurt you.

I learned about drugs in school and ran away from home. I had been gone for 4 months, without so much as a call to let my parents know that I was safe. I had met a truck driver on the road and stayed with him in Pennsylvania. I began to miss my family and finally called my brother I told him that I loved him and he told me I did not love anyone but myself. I decided it was time to go home and give everything to God because he was the only one who could help me.

When I arrived home, I felt like the prodigal son. My parents had welcomed me back with open arms letting me know how much they loved me and wanted me. I had been afraid they would be mad at me yet it was exactly the opposite.

My mom got me a job at a printing company where she was working. That is where I met Arnold. He was funny but I thought he was not my type. He had bright red hair and wore thick glasses. He was driving the delivery truck. His mother worked there too and her and I would sit in her car to smoke during the breaks. I enjoyed being with her.

One day Arnold asked me to go on a date with him he said we could go out the next week and see a movie called 'Take this job and shove it." I called my friend that night and she and I went and watched it. I did not want to go out with Arnold. I told my mom that he was not my type and it would not be good for us to go out. My mom loved him and thought he would be a good choice for me.

Therefore, the next week I told him that I had already seen that movie. I thought he would just say okay maybe some other time but no, he said we could go see a different movie. So we went out to dinner and then to a movie. As we were walking out to the car, he asked me if he could hold my hand. I told him no it hurt. I did not want to hold his hand. I did not even like him other than he was funny and told good jokes and he did make me laugh but I did not like him at all for a relationship.

He started coming to church with me and soon we were around each other all the time. I was beginning to like him a lot.

We had been together several months when we decided it was time. So we agreed and we had sex in the back of his station wagon. I thought I found someone to love. When I got home after we had sex I had emotions in my head that I had never had before. I did not understand them and did not know if I liked them.

Sometimes Arnold had temper problems and he would become angry. I could make him laugh and he would get out of his bad mood.

My cousin was in town visiting and she was the first one I told. She just said wow I hope you do not get pregnant. I said me too. The next day I remember feeling nauseous and I wondered if I was already pregnant. No way I could not be we only had sex one time. That night Arnold and I went out and I told him that I felt bad about what happened and we should not do it again until we got married. We both agreed that was the best thing for both of us.

Two weeks later I was still feeling nauseous so I told my mother I thought I might be pregnant. She took me to Birthright where my aunt worked and we took a pregnancy test. Sure enough, I was pregnant. I could not believe it how could I get pregnant after only one time?

Joanna

CHAPTER 21

I had to tell Arnold. He called to find out what the test showed and I told him that he had to come over so we could talk in person. He came over and I believed we were going to be okay. He said he would marry me and take care of the baby.

We went over to his house to tell his parents the news. He did not think his dad would have a problem with it but he knew his mom would since he had been so close to his mother. His mother wanted to have a meeting with my mom, Arnold and me. We scheduled it and I cooked breakfast for all of us for this meeting.

We ate our breakfast and everyone sat around in the living room. Arnold's mom said we could not get married. Arnold had to finish high school and she told me she did not believe the baby was Arnold's anyway. I said yes it was Arnold's I had menstruated 3 months in a row before we had sex and I knew I could not be pregnant before then. She wanted proof that it was Arnold's since I was already showing after only 3 weeks. I could not understand it but I was getting very big very fast.

I sobbed so hard that I thought I was going to loose my baby. I went to the backyard of my house and sat up on the freezer we had on the back porch. Arnold came around the house and found me out there crying. He put his arms around me and informed me it would be all right that we could just elope and not worry about the family.

Arnold and I were seeing each other every night talking and trying to sort through all this and trying to figure out what we needed to do. Sometimes we would fight about it he told me he wanted me to have an abortion. I could not do that as my moral beliefs would not allow that. He would become very angry and tear up the lawn when he drove off.

The decision in front of us was a huge decision. Sometimes we talked about just getting married and this being a good thing for us. We would get a small house and start our family.

My parents knew what a struggle I was going through at that time and thought it would be best for me to get away for a few days and stay with my brother who was living in Dallas.

I tried to call Arnold before I left but he had already gone to bed. I told his mother that I was leaving town and would be back soon. She would not wake him up to talk to me on the telephone. My dad and I left to go to Dallas. I decided that if Arnold would come down and get me then we should be married.

He came down after about 4 days to pick me up. When we got back to the city we broke up.

The stress was too much. I decided to move in with my grandparents and get a job as a waitress.

Arnold and I agreed that he would go to the doctor with me, as he wanted to be a part of the baby's life even if we decided not to get married.

In December 1981 we went to the doctor and she informed us that I was only too large for my gestation and she wanted to perform an ultrasound to find out if I was having twins. Arnold and I laughed about the thought and he mentioned something about how much child support he would have to pay if he had two babies instead of one.

The doctor scheduled the ultrasound and we went to the hospital where it was scheduled. As I lay there on the table the technician asked us why we needed an ultrasound. Arnold and I laughed as we told her that the doctor thought I might be having twins. She said well there is one baby and she moved the scope and said there's the other baby. I looked at Arnold as he turned white.

We were having twins. I was not married, how was I to care for two babies when the fear of having only one baby was almost more than I could handle. I was only 16 years old. I was not married. My class had not even graduated. What was I going to do.

When we left the hospital, we drove home in silence listening only to Pat Benatar sing "Hell is for Children."

We married on January 28, 1982 in the breakroom at his work. Arnold's boss was an ordained minister and offered to perform the wedding ceremony. On March 15, 1982 I gave birth to twin boys. I felt my life had just begun. I could overlook all of Arnold's anger outbursts when I saw those beautiful boys.

As I thought about all the memories through my life with Arnold and my children. I could not help but remember the love that I had hoped for in my home. All the times that we laughed, all the plans that we had made for our lives were gone. I was alone with no mate to share memories with, alone with an empty bed, alone with no shoulder to cry on, but also alone with nobody to hurt me any more.

As all of the thoughts went through my head the resounding of music came to my head. I begun to sing songs I had not sang or heard in a long time. I was free from the abuse I had endured off and on for so many years. I drove home and sang, "Oh For a Thousand Tongues to Sing", and "I've Got a Mansion Over the Hilltop." I could not help but think of my friend and mentor Bro. Eddis, who was in Heaven and thank him for all the support and wisdom he had shared with me throughout my marriage. I knew he was not looking down on me with as he was celebrating his own triumph. He was with Jesus away from all the troubles of the earth. I still thought of him and wondered if he would be proud that I stood up or if he would be disappointed in my decision. I always wanted to know that he would be proud.

I knew that Bro. Eddis wanted me to move on with my life and make a better life for myself so I began thinking of what I should do. I needed to go back to college and finish my Bachelor's Degree.

My decisions were mine and I was going to deal with the problem directly and make something meaningful of my life. It was my life and I did not have to question my actions because of other people around me. I was the maker of my destiny from now on and what a destiny I would make. I could actually smile without feeling like I was dying on the inside because now I was smiling with my entire being.

Smile When You Feel Like Dying

Joanna

Smile When You Feel Like Dying

Joanna

www.ingramcontent.com/pod-product-compliance
Lightning Source LLC
Chambersburg PA
CBHW051835040426
42447CB00006B/542